# A Note to Parents & Teachers—

Welcome to I See Trucks from Xist Publishing! These books are designed to inspire discovery and delight in the youngest readers. Each book features very simple sentences with visual cues to help beginners read their very first text.

You can help each child develop a lifetime love of reading right from the very start. Here are some ways to help a beginning reader get going:

- Read the book aloud as a first introduction
- Run your fingers below the words as you read each line
- Give the child the chance to finish the sentences or read repeating words while you read the rest.
- Encourage the child to read aloud every day!

Published proudly in the State of Texas, USA by Xist Publishing
www.xistpublishing.com
24200 Southwest Freeway Suite 402- 290 Rosenberg, TX 77471
All images licensed from Adobe Stock
First Edition

Hardcover ISBN: 978-1-5324-5461-5
Saddle Stitch ISBN: 978-1-5324-5558-2
Perfect Bound ISBN: 978-1-5324-5462-2
eISBN: 978-1-5324-5460-8

PUBLISHED IN TEXAS

# I S👓e Trucks
# Dump
# Truck

written by **August Hoeft**

x*ist Publishing

INSPIRING DISCOVERY & DELIGHT

# I see a dump truck.

# The dump truck is red.

The dump truck has a bed that dumps.

The dump truck holds rocks.

# The dump truck helps move dirt.

# I see a dump truck.

# Things to do next!

## Write a Sentence

I see a _____.

## Drawing

Make a drawing of your favorite truck.

## Sharing

Talk to your classmates about your favorite picture in this book. Explain to them why you like it.

# WORD LIST

| | |
|---|---|
| a | is |
| bed | move |
| dirt | red |
| dump | rocks |
| dumps | see |
| has | that |
| helps | the |
| holds | truck |
| I | |

www.ingramcontent.com/pod-product-compliance
Lightning Source LLC
LaVergne TN
LVHW010320090426
835508LV00053B/3408